M000191148

Oct 31, 09

Dear Katie & Tim

Thanks for all your
help & great
friendship.

Love,
Mick

Princeton
History and Architecture

Marilyn Menago

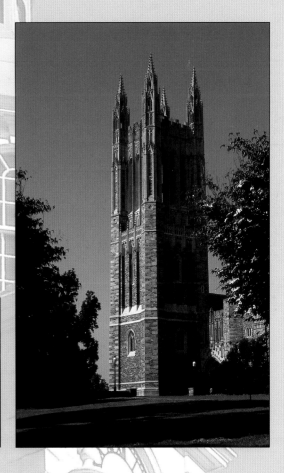

Schiffer Publishing Ltd

4880 Lower Valley Road Atglen, Pennsylvania 19310

Dedication

To Bob, Scott, Sharon, and Sean, with all my love.

Other Schiffer Books on Related Subjects
Timeless Architecture: Homes of Distinction by Harrison Design Associates, by Elizabeth Merideth Dowling
Cape May Point: The Illustrated History from 1875 to the Present, by Joe Jordan
Jersey City: A Monumental History, by Randall Gabrielan

Copyright © 2007 by Marilyn Menago
Library of Congress Control Number: 2007921518

All rights reserved. No part of this work may be reproduced or used in any form or by any means—graphic, electronic, or mechanical, including photocopying or information storage and retrieval systems—without written permission from the publisher.

The scanning, uploading and distribution of this book or any part thereof via the Internet or via any other means without the permission of the publisher is illegal and punishable by law. Please purchase only authorized editions and do not participate in or encourage the electronic piracy of copyrighted materials.

"Schiffer," "Schiffer Publishing Ltd. & Design," and the "Design of pen and ink well" are registered trademarks of Schiffer Publishing Ltd.

Designed by Mark David Bowyer
Type set in Bodoni Bd BT / Adobe Jensen Pro BT

ISBN: 978-0-7643-2626-4
Printed in China

Published by Schiffer Publishing Ltd.
4880 Lower Valley Road
Atglen, PA 19310
Phone: (610) 593-1777; Fax: (610) 593-2002
E-mail: Info@schifferbooks.com

For the largest selection of fine reference books on this and related subjects, please visit our web site at **www.schifferbooks.com**
We are always looking for people to write books on new and related subjects. If you have an idea for a book please contact us at the above address.

This book may be purchased from the publisher.
Include $3.95 for shipping.
Please try your bookstore first.
You may write for a free catalog.

In Europe, Schiffer books are distributed by
Bushwood Books
6 Marksbury Ave.
Kew Gardens
Surrey TW9 4JF England
Phone: 44 (0) 20 8392-8585; Fax: 44 (0) 20 8392-9876
E-mail: info@bushwoodbooks.co.uk
Website: www.bushwoodbooks.co.uk
Free postage in the U.K., Europe; air mail at cost.

Contents

Acknowledgments

I am deeply grateful to all librarians, historians, curators, and administrators who assisted me in locating information, escorted me around their property, and took the time to answer my incessant questions: Maureen Smyth and Eileen Morales of the Princeton Historical Society; Michelle Roemer-Schoen of Princeton Theological Seminary; Margaret Sullivan of the Institute for Advanced Study; Beverly Mills of Drumthwacket; Clare Smith and Anne Gossen of Morven; Peggy Carlson of Rockingham; and especially Tom Bartus of Princeton University. Without their help, valuable pieces of information would be missing. My sincere thanks as well to all the academic institutions, which graciously complied in allowing their eminent schools to be photographed, and to all the homeowners who permitted me to traipse on their lawns, tripod in hand.

I especially want to thank my editors, Tina Skinner, who patiently ignored my missed deadlines and gently prodded me to continue, and Donna Baker, who made invaluable corrections and additions to the text; Bruce Waters and Mark Bowyer, whose designs brought the book together; my daughter, Sharon Cost, for all her work on the map and not complaining about the changes; my son, Sean, for all his time spent reading and editing the text; my son, Scott, for his sage accounting advice; and last, but not least, a deep indebtedness goes to my husband Bob, whose support and encouragement was tenfold throughout this project.

Introduction

"I am privileged to live here in Princeton as if on an island that in many respects resembles the charming palace garden in Liken. Into this small university town, too, the chaotic voices of human strife barely penetrate. I am almost ashamed to be living in such peace while all the rest struggle and suffer."

—*Albert Einstein to Queen Elizabeth of Belgium*

Princeton is often referred to as the quintessential university town, yet it is actually so much more than that. Princeton's importance and contribution to the history of New Jersey is great enough for the town to stand on its own. After I was approached to photograph Princeton, I made a mental checklist of how I would approach my assignment. I could not foresee that when seeking information for the photo captions I would end up devoting so much time to Princeton's history, despite my love of the subject. This was supposed to be a photographic study only. Nonetheless, I spent many hours at Bainbridge House, headquarters of Princeton Historical Society, becoming totally engrossed and obsessed with the narrative aspect of the project.

My research began with Constance Greiff's *Princeton Architecture*, a very informative source on the architecture and beginnings of Princeton. As I roamed the streets seeking out the notable architecture Greiff showcased, however, I soon discovered that quite a few of those venerable buildings had been destroyed since her 1967 publication—many of them still in their prime. The town's strong preservation advocacy notwithstanding, Princeton sometimes lost out to more powerful groups with opposing ideas. Statewide, as well, many buildings of historical and architectural importance have succumbed to the ubiquitous New Jersey bulldozer.

Through my photographs, I hope to portray the charm and uniqueness of Princeton as developed by its history and diverse architecture, as well as to inspire others to preserve America's past—not just in Princeton but everywhere. By viewing our nation's rich legacy through its public buildings and homes, a window into the past is glimpsed. Historic preservation enriches the community by ensuring a visual education to residents and visitors alike. I hope that those visiting Princeton—whether in person or via armchair—will find this apparent, although there are many fine homes and public buildings I was not able to capture on film. Despite this, I believe Princeton's character is obvious.

After more than two years of scouring for images that depict the essence of Princeton, it was hard to say goodbye. I have come to love Princeton and now think of this lovely town as my own.

—Marilyn Menago
Monroe Township, New Jersey

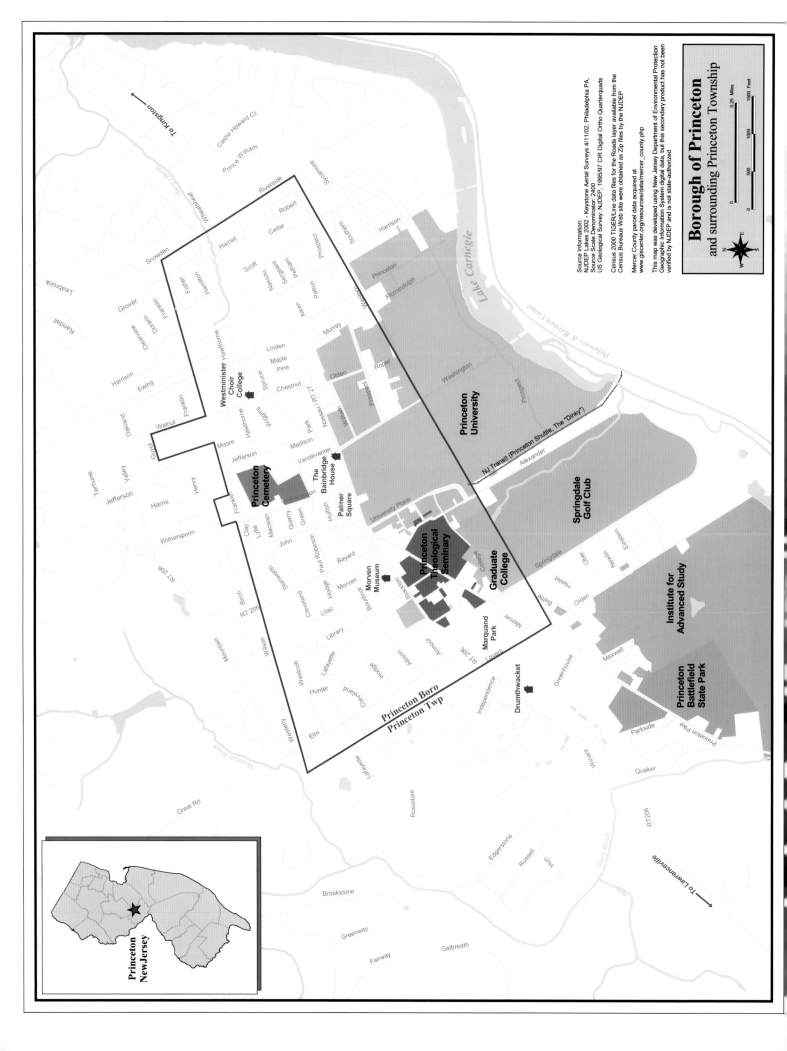

Borough of Princeton
and surrounding Princeton Township

Source Information:
NJDEP Lakes 2002 - Keystone Aerial Surveys 4/11/02, Philadelphia PA,
Source Scale Denominator: 2400
US Geological Survey: NJDEP, 1995/97 CIR Digital Ortho Quarterquads

Census 2000 TIGER/Line data files for the Roads layer available from the
Census Bureaus Web site were obtained as Zip files by the NJDEP

Mercer County parcel data acquired at
www.giscenter.org/resources/data/mercer_county.php

This map was developed using New Jersey Department of Environmental Protection
Geographic Information System digital data, but this secondary product has not been
verified by NJDEP and is not state-authorized

Princeton
New Jersey

A Village Grows

Driving into Princeton on Washington Road, passing by one-hundred-year-old American elm trees that proudly line the avenue, one senses the bucolic Princeton of long ago. Vacant fields lie behind the stately elms, evoking images of old farms that once dotted the countryside. As soccer fields suddenly appear on the right, followed by Princeton University's boathouse on the left, the nostalgic spell is broken—replaced by anticipation of the world-renowned academic institutions that lie ahead. Princeton is a vibrant university town with a shopping district that features designer clothing stores, trendy boutiques, bookstores, coffee houses, cafés, and restaurants all standing alongside the local pharmacy, the barber shop, and dry cleaners. On the fringes of the shopping area lies a bedroom community of stately mansions ensconced on tree-lined streets, some partially hidden behind stone walls, some not seen at all, but all announcing an affluent population. Princeton's beginnings, however, were as humble as that of most Colonial towns in the seventeenth century.

View from Princeton University's boathouse of Washington Road Bridge where it crosses Lake Carnegie. Washington Road runs through Princeton University's campus and ends at Nassau Street.

Washington Road Elm Allee, one of the loveliest roads traveling into any town, leads into Princeton under a canopy of one hundred-year-old American elm trees. Because of a proposed plan to extend Route 1, it was put on New Jersey's endangered sites list in 2000. It is now on the National Register of Historic Places, and as of this writing, there are alternative proposals to alleviate the Route 1 traffic problem.

According to the Worlidge Map of 1687-1691, Henry Greenland was the first property owner within the boundaries of Princeton Township. After purchasing two hundred acres in 1683 along the Millstone River near Kingston, he opened his home as a tavern, portions of which survive in the Greenland-Brinson-Gulick house. Greenland's only neighbor was his son-in-law, Daniel Brinson, whose land was located between Springdale and Washington Roads. In the 1690s, several Quaker families bought land owned by William Penn that was situated between Millstone River and Stony Brook, not far from the King's Highway (today's Rt. 27 and part of Rt. 206). Twenty-five years later, William Potts built two gristmills and a bolting mill by the Stony Brook Bridge, establishing Stony Brook as a vital community. The early settlers were yeoman of the middling class, also skilled in trades they employed when not working their farm. Among this group of enterprising farmer-carpenters, -tailors, -coopers, and -tanners, were the Oldens and Stocktons, whose families would later prosper to lead Princeton both socially and politically. In 1724, Stony Brook village was renamed Prince Town in honor of England's Prince William of Orange and Nassau.

The only road into Prince Town from either New York or Philadelphia was the heavily trafficked King's Highway, which brought many prominent travelers and visitors to the area. During the American Revolution, patriots such as George Washington, John Adams, Paul Revere, John Paul Jones, Thomas Paine, and the French liaisons rode into the village to discuss the rebellion, filling the many inns and taverns. Since Princeton's location on the King's Highway was halfway between New York and Philadelphia, it became the overnight stagecoach stop by the middle of the eighteenth century. A number of taverns or inns became known for their superior accommodations, food, and entertainment, making Princeton a welcome layover for weary passengers. Taverns also comprised a social hub for the locals, who gathered there to gossip with each other and to glean outside news from travelers. At that time, taverns throughout the colonies were mostly established in homes, rather than in buildings erected specifically for that purpose. After the College of New Jersey (now Princeton University) moved to the village in 1756, more taverns were built to accommodate the increased influx of visitors. Soon a village grew up around this cottage industry. Lawyers, physicians, and merchants that administered to the everyday needs of a community followed, creating a town center along today's Nassau Street.

The original farming community of Stony Brook remained and continued to prosper. Farm settlements that spread around the countryside at the beginning of the eighteenth century eventually circumscribed the village center. As prosperity mushroomed, so did the size of the homes. Additions were added on to the original one- and two-room houses to emulate the Georgian manor homes prevalent in Philadelphia and Virginia. Many of these noble farmhouses are extant today, although most have been extensively altered. By the end of the eighteenth century, town citizens wanted to incorporate Princeton as a larger municipality, but Stony Brook residents objected. In 1813, the borough was incorporated (it became autonomous and a separate entity in 1894), but the surrounding township's boundary lines were not drawn until 1838.

After the Revolution, Princeton's growth continued, partly because of its reputation as a premier stagecoach stop. With construction in the 1830s of both a nearby canal that flowed alongside the Millstone River (part of which is now Carnegie Lake) and railroad lines that ran into town, Princeton's new modes of transportation further encouraged prosperity. The town's boom was also fostered by the Col-

Quaker Joseph Worth built the Worth-Bauer Homestead in early 1700. A portion of the rear wing is attributed to the original house. The present house was built in 1815, either to replace or add onto the first house. In 1715, Worth purchased a gristmill, later known as Worth's Mill, which remained in the family and in continuous use until the early twentieth century.

lege of New Jersey, which focused on elevating the school to compete on international levels, and the arrival of the Theological Seminary. Princeton's renowned reputation for higher learning brought other academic institutions into the area that, in turn, lured scholars, scientists, statesmen, and writers from around the world—James Madison, Woodrow Wilson, Grover Cleveland, Albert Einstein, Robert Oppenheimer, T.S. Eliot, F. Scott Fitzgerald, and Paul Robeson (who was born in Princeton), to name just a few. Many of them, including Presidents Wilson and Cleveland, have at one time made Princeton their home.

Today, Princeton has three preeminent higher learning institutions, a world-renowned choir college, a boy's choir school, excellent secondary schools, an educational testing service, a public opinion polling center, research centers, training centers, a premier performing arts center, and numerous major corporations. Bus and train service to New York is available, as is as an airport for those in a hurry. Yet despite the hustle and bustle of Nassau Street, Princeton still exudes an aura of "Small Town America" that captures our hearts, delights our senses, and enlivens our imagination with glimpses of times gone by.

Farmer Aaron Hewes originally built Maybury Hill (c.1725). Aaron's son, Joseph, born here in 1730, later moved to North Carolina. As a delegate of that state, he was one of the signers of the Declaration of Independence.

The kitchen wing of Mansgrove (c.1722) was typical of an eighteenth-century tenant farm; the delicate Federal details of the main section, however, indicate an early nineteenth-century structure. Mansgrove represents the type of upper class farm that was burgeoning in the eighteenth century.

Castle Howard's origins are somewhat uncertain. It is known, however, that the main section of the house was erected c.1760. Capt. Howard, a British army officer, was a patriot sympathizer who, it has been said, wrote "No Tory talk here" over the mantle. The Greek Revival elements to the front were added in the mid-nineteenth century. An addition in the back was the private "pad" of Hobey Baker, a 1914 hockey and football star for Princeton, while his parents owned the home.

The interior of the Gulick-Hodge-Scott House's left wing contains elements of a pre-Revolutionary home. The brick section in the center has larger windows and delicate details, however, indicating that it was built in the early nineteenth century.

Bainbridge House (c.1766), at 158 Nassau Street, is the head-quarters of the Historical Society of Princeton, which leases the building from Princeton University for one dollar annually. It was built by Job Stockton, a descendant of one of the founding families of Princeton. Despite various uses throughout the years, Bainbridge has retained its original Georgian integrity, including the interior staircase and paneled walls. The Historical Society keeps a fifteen-hundred-volume library and maintains a period museum.

Beatty House (c.1780), was originally built on Nassau Street across from Bainbridge House. The house welcomed the Marquis de Lafayette as an overnight guest in 1825. James Vandeventer, a local merchant, moved the house in 1875 to its present location at 19 Vandeventer Avenue.

Charles Smith Olden, New Jersey's governor during the Civil War, built Drumthwacket in 1836. A Princeton native, Olden returned to his roots after attaining considerable wealth in New Orleans. Located at 344 Stockton Street, Drumthwacket has been the permanent residence of New Jersey governors since 1981. The pink ribbons on the columns represent the Susan G. Komen Breast Cancer Foundation. Many civic groups and charities are welcome here.

Statuary in Drumthwacket's
lovely garden.

Woodrow Wilson House, 72 Library Place. Built in 1836 by Charles Steadman, the home was occupied by Wilson and his wife in 1889 when he became a faculty member at Princeton University.

Albert Einstein lived in this house while he was Director of the School of Mathematics at the Institute for Advanced Study from 1935 until his death in 1955. Built in the Greek Revival style in 1840 by Samuel Stevens, the house originally stood on Alexander Street. It was moved to its present site at 112 Mercer Street in 1875.

Westland (c.1854). Grover Cleveland and his wife purchased this house in 1896 and named it for Dean West of the Graduate College. Cleveland's close relationship with undergraduates made Westlawn a haven for them. On the 18th of March, Cleveland's birthday, students would march by the house at 15 Hodge Road in celebration.

Sheldon House. In 1868, Rev. George Sheldon, a resident of Princeton, inherited the family house located in Northampton, Massachusetts. Not wanting to move there, he simply transported the house by barge through New England and New York waterways to the Delaware and Raritan Canal, where it finally came to rest at 10 Mercer Street. Today, the quintessential Greek Revival home houses the Bonner Foundation, a privately funded scholarship program.

Built in 1913 by Guy R. McLane in memory of his wife, Dorothea's House opened in 1914 as a community center for Italian immigrants. Located at 120 John Street, it now serves as an Italian-American cultural center providing programs such as Italian language classes and scholarships.

Before it was moved to its present location at 20 Bayard Lane in 1875, the Peacock Inn stood at the corner of Nassau Street and University Place. It is a much-altered eighteenth-century house originally owned by Jonathan Deare, a prominent patriot. In 1911, the property became an inn welcoming the likes of F. Scott Fitzgerald, Albert Einstein, and Bertrand Russell. Today, it is the only bed and breakfast in downtown Princeton.

A professor at the Princeton Theological Seminary built this house, located at 6 Mercer Street, on his father-in-law's abandoned site in 1814; on this property had stood the only structure in Princeton to be burned to the ground by the British. The Nassau Club, a social organization formed in 1889 by members of the faculty, alumni, and residents of the town, purchased the house in 1903. The club provides dining, lodging, lectures, and social events for its members.

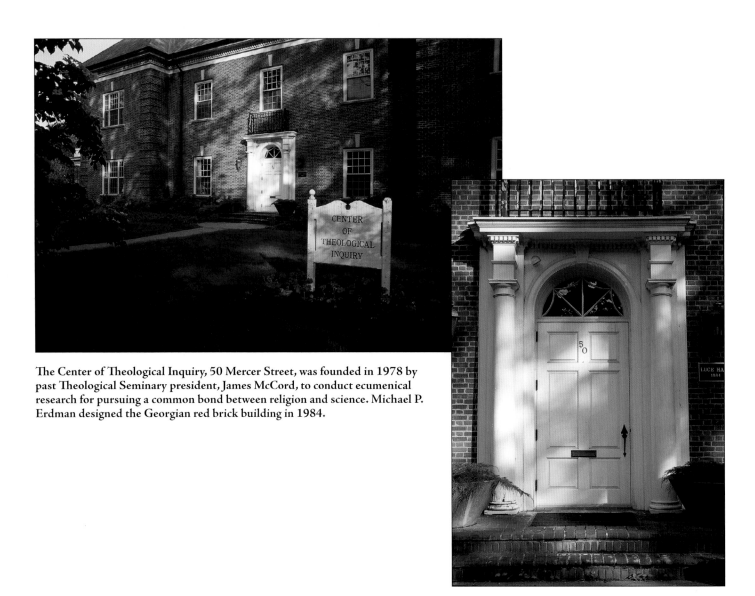

The Center of Theological Inquiry, 50 Mercer Street, was founded in 1978 by past Theological Seminary president, James McCord, to conduct ecumenical research for pursuing a common bond between religion and science. Michael P. Erdman designed the Georgian red brick building in 1984.

Thomas N. McCarter donated funds in 1929 to build a theatre for the Princeton University Triangle Club. On opening night of February 21, 1930, McCarter Theatre saw a young sophomore named Jimmy Stewart in its chorus. For the next two decades, McCarter ran pre-Broadway shows that starred Katherine Hepburn, Helen Hayes, the Barrymores, and the Lunts. Although McCarter has been controlled by the McCarter Theatre Company since 1973, the Triangle Club still stages student run performances there twice a year. Always expanding, McCarter's newest addition is the Berlind Theatre.

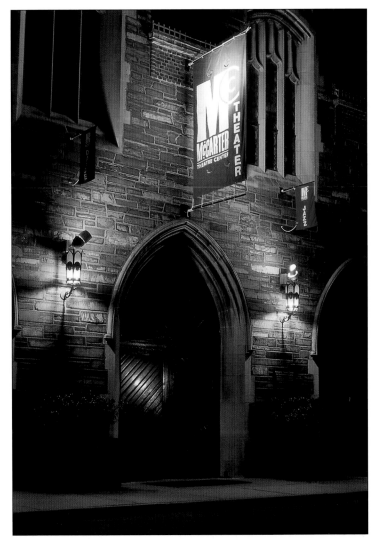

Performances and productions are run throughout the year at McCarter, 91 University Place, whose excellent reputation has been highly rewarded; in 1994, it won a Tony for Outstanding Regional Theatre in the country.

Completed in 2002 and the recipient of several awards in 2003, Princeton Township Municipal Building is an L-shaped, four-story structure containing 55,000 square feet.

Princeton Public Library, Princeton's newest project, opened on April 24, 2004. Designed by Hillier Architecture and located on Witherspoon Street, the library's 55,000 square feet of space and 10,500 square feet of glass are contained within three floors. It has the capacity for 175,000 books, and more than 100 computers are available for public use.

Princeton Railroad Station. Originally, the railroad line went into downtown. In 1867, the main station was moved to Princeton Junction, but a shuttle (now called "the Dinky") was provided to bring students to the area of the Princeton University Store. After Blair Hall was built in 1918, the train station was moved back to its present location.

"The Princeton Bell," located outside the Borough Hall steps, was especially cast for the U.S.S. *Princeton*, which was commanded by Princeton native, Captain Robert F. Stockton.

Princeton Cemetery reads like a who's who. Aaron Burr, Sr. and Jr., Jonathan Edwards, John Witherspoon, Grover Cleveland, Paul Tulane, and a number of Princeton University presidents all lie beneath the ground here.

Grover Cleveland gravesite.

Antique and boutique stores line up on Chambers Street.

Originally part of the Assanpink Trail, Nassau Street was once a narrow path used by the Lenni Lenape Indians. Through the years it has been known by many names, including King's Highway.

Lower Pyne and Upper Pyne (the latter demolished in 1964) were gifts to Princeton University in 1896 by Moses Taylor Pyne. Located opposite Nassau Hall, each building's upper floor housed a dormitory of twenty students while the ground floor was leased out to shops. The students moved out in 1950 when housing on campus became more plentiful. Today, Lower Pyne is privately owned.

Today, Nassau Street is part of the Lincoln High-way that runs through the center of town. Its variety of establishments attracts both locals and visitors.

Downstairs in the Nassau Inn is the Yankee Doodle Tap Room, where you can enjoy a pint and see memorabilia salvaged from the original tavern—photographs, tables covered with initials and dates, a fireplace presented by the class of 1912. Norman Rockwell painted the sign for the Tap Room.

Nassau Inn. In 1769, the latest owner of this c.1757 house opened it as the College Inn, where students and Revolutionary War advocates that included George Washington, Paul Revere, and Thomas Paine gathered to discuss events. In the early eighteenth century, new owners changed the name to Nassau Inn and it continued to operate as such until 1937, when it was destroyed along with other shops to make way for Palmer Square. Today's Nassau Inn is a colonial replica, with a modern wing that contains over two hundred guest rooms along with numerous banquet rooms serving the needs of Princeton's thriving corporate community.

Nassau Inn at Christmas.

Over eighty years old, Cox's Market on Nassau Street is the oldest food establishment in Princeton. Prior to housing the market, the building was home to a speakeasy during Prohibition.

Palmer Square. In 1937, Edgar Palmer financed Palmer Square to revitalize downtown Princeton. Several old venerable buildings, including the original Nassau Inn, were razed to make room for the square that would be surrounded by shops and open space, with the new Nassau Inn as its centerpiece. Designed by architect Thomas Stapleton, Palmer Square followed the Colonial Revival movement that began after the restoration of Williamsburg. The square was not fully completed until the 1980s.

Colonial Musketeers Fife and Drum Corps from Hackettstown march in the Memorial Day parade on Nassau Street.

Witherspoon Street, located off Nassau Street, has many fine restaurants and specialty shops.

Begun in 1830, the Delaware-Raritan Canal was an important trade route, peaking in the 1860s and 1870s. Princeton's portion, which runs for over six miles, can be used for recreational purposes as well as providing a water supply for Princeton and neighboring towns. A path, which runs alongside the entire canal, is used for walking, biking, and in certain areas, horseback riding.

Originally part of the 30-acre estate of Guernsey Hall, Marquand Park features seventeen acres of woodlands, forest glades, and open parkland, which contains many specimen trees. Every spring, the glade bursts forth with a riot of white wildflowers. The children's playground is busy most of the year.

Harrison Street Bridge crosses Lake Carnegie.

Damming the Millstone River and Stony Brook confluence at Kingston in 1906 created Lake Carnegie, which is 800 feet across at its widest and runs three and a half miles long. Princeton University's crew teams practice their sport on the lake and Princeton residents fish and canoe there.

Houses of Worship

Nassau Presbyterian Church, 61 Nassau Street. The congregation of the First Presbyterian Church, founded in 1766, has met continuously on this site. The original building was a plain brick meeting house with its side facing the street. After surviving destruction from the Revolutionary War, it burned to the ground in 1813, then again in 1835. A year later, Charles Steadman, using a plan he purchased from Philadelphia architect Thomas U. Walter, erected the Greek Revival church that stands today.

Trinity Church, 33 Mercer Street. When a larger church was needed, Richard M. Upjohn, son of the architect of New York's Trinity Church, employed both Gothic Revival and Romanesque Revival elements to design this edifice in 1868; the Parish House was built in 1894. In 1914-1915, architect Ralph Adams Cram added the stone choir and sanctuary. There are several entrances into the church.

Princeton United Methodist Church, Nassau Street and Vandeventer Avenue. Founded in 1847, the church's original two-story
brick building was dedicated in 1849. The present structure
replaced it in 1911 on land donated by Moses Taylor Pyne and was
designed in the Collegiate Gothic style that so impressed Pyne.
The beautiful stained glass windows are a highlight of the church;
especially so is the original Tiffany in St. George's Sanctuary.

Nassau Christian Center, 26 Nassau Street. Originally the Second Presbyterian Church, this Gothic church was constructed in 1868 after both the First Church and the old Second Church were at full capacity. It became the preferred church of employee Presbyterians, while employers attended the First Church. Nassau Christian Center purchased the building in 1973 when the two Presbyterian churches merged. For three seasons of the year, the front of the church is a riot of color.

Right:
First Church of Christ Scientist, 16 Bayard Lane. The local congregation built their church in 1949; it has recently been restored to its original appearance. Periodically, Albert Einstein attended services here.

St. Paul's Roman Catholic Church, 214 Nassau Street. The first Catholic chaplain came to Princeton in 1795, privately ministering to the French émigrés in their homes. An old farmhouse served as the first permanent location for worship. When the congregation grew, a small modest church was erected on Nassau Street with a school in the basement and a small rectory. In 1857, a small frame church was built on the present site; in 1957, the present Gothic Revival church replaced it.

Right:
The Aquinas Institute has occupied this 1907 home at 65 Stockton Street since 1953. Although the Institute is not part of the university, religious services are provided for students, faculty, and staff. Prior to Aquinas's use of the home, Thomas Mann, winner of the 1929 Nobel Prize in Literature, lived here from 1938 to 1941 while he was a guest lecturer at the university.

First Baptist Church, John Street and Paul Robeson Place. After meeting in worshipers' homes and the Odd Fellow Hall for five years, the Bright Hope Baptist Church purchased land and built their church in 1885. It was renamed in 1930.

Witherspoon Street Presbyterian Church, 112 Witherspoon Street. Originally known as the First Presbyterian Church of Color, it was created when members of the First Presbyterian Church (now Nassau Presbyterian Church) left to establish their own house of worship in 1837. Reverend William Drew Robeson, Paul Robeson's father, was minister at Witherspoon from 1880 to 1901.

The Glorious Cause

For over two centuries, scholars of the American Revolution have attributed the victories at Trenton and Princeton as the turning point of the Revolutionary War. Preceding these battles, desertion among the militia and apathy among the colonists had been increasing at an alarming rate. During the summer and fall of 1776, initial war fervor began to wane after Washington's humiliating defeats in New York sent the General and his army retreating across New Jersey into Pennsylvania. After the win at Princeton, however, it no longer seemed impossible that the Americans could beat the invincible British army.

From the onset of dissension with England to the first congress held by the new United States of America, the small country village of Princeton played a significant role in our country's early history. On June 22, 1776, New Jersey's new Provincial Congress sent five delegates to the Continental Congress in Philadelphia. They included two Princetonians, both strong proponents of liberty and supporters of the Glorious Cause: John Witherspoon, president of the College of New Jersey, and Richard Stockton, a brilliant lawyer considered to be one of the wealthiest men in New Jersey. This act would put both men in jeopardy, particularly Stockton, as they were now considered enemies of England. When the British invaded Princeton in November 1776 and seized Nassau Hall as well as private homes and churches, both men fled with their families. Richard and Annis Stockton went to Monmouth County to stay with friends. Soon after, a group of Tories dragged Richard from his bed and imprisoned him with the British at Perth Amboy, where he received brutal treatment. He would be released in early January of 1777, after signing an "Obedience to His Majesty" oath in exchange for a full pardon and his family's safekeeping. This act tarnished Richard's reputation, but ill feelings towards him softened after a time. He died four years later in February 1781 from cancer.

The British occupation of Princeton did not last long, after events finally turned in favor of the patriots. On the morning of December 26, Washington and his troops crossed the Delaware River from Pennsylvania and overcame the Hessians at Trenton. After the surprise attack, the British in Princeton awaited additional troops that were needed to strengthen their garrison. When General Charles Cornwallis and his army arrived on the first of January, they immediately pushed towards Trenton along the King's Highway, reaching the town at dusk. Under cover of darkness that night, Washington moved his army around the sleeping British and headed towards Princeton, leaving a small group of men at Trenton as a decoy. Cornwallis, hearing sounds at the enemy's camp, went to sleep confident that Washington could wait until morning. When he awoke to learn that the "old fox" had outsmarted him, Cornwallis rounded up his men and charged back to Princeton.

Meanwhile, the stealthy American troops reached Princeton just after dawn. Unfortunately, their plan to attack the British rear guard was discovered, which forced a change in their strategy. On January 3, Washington's enormous presence and courage on the field spurred his men on to victory, despite the change of plans. The fierce battle resulted in one hundred British casualties and forty American, including Scottish-born American officer, Brigadier General Hugh Mercer, who died from his wounds nine days later. From the first shots to the last, the entire battle—ranging from Stony Brook village to the college campus—was over in forty-five minutes. Although the conflict was brief, historians consider the battle at Princeton to be one of the fiercest in the entire war. After it was over, the Continental troops moved into Princeton, and upon several attacks the British fled Nassau Hall, which remained in American hands until the war's conclusion.

Princeton suffered extensive damage from both British and American occupations, with the Presbyterian Church and the college sustaining the greatest destruction and pillage. For most of the Revolution, Nassau Hall had been occupied by British and American troops for use as a barracks or hospital, as well as a stable for horses. At the end of the war, the interior was in such a shambles that it took several years to be completely restored. The entire contents of the library had been burned for fuel; math and scientific instruments were completely destroyed. Quick renovations, however, allowed the fledgling Congress to make Nassau Hall the first capital building of the nascent United States of America.

In June of 1783, the Continental Congress adjourned and moved out of Philadelphia when angry Pennsylvania troops marched towards the city to demand back pay. On June 26, Congress reconvened in the renovated library of Nassau Hall, establishing Princeton as the capital of the new nation. Elias Boudinot, President of the Continental Congress and a native of Princeton, made his official residence Morven, the home of his widowed sister, Annis Stockton. The heretofore-quiet Princeton bustled with events and activities. The French Ambassador, Chevalier de la Luzerne, attended the Fourth of July celebration, and the Dutch Minister, Peter Johannes van Berckel, arrived to present his credentials to Congress. The Netherlands was the first nation other than France to recognize the new country. In August, George and Martha Washington took up residence in Rockingham, the home of a widow at nearby Rocky Hill. It was on the second floor of Rockingham that the general crafted his *Farewell Orders to the Armies of the United States*, giving thanks and praise to his troops. During Washington's stay, Congress invited him to Nassau Hall to honor him for his successful campaign in fighting for independence. Town residents, to show their gratitude, bestowed lavish dinners and banquets on the Washingtons.

But the festivities eventually came to an end. Princeton was too small and too rustic to remain the nation's capital for long. The seventy or so houses, together with the town's superior inns and taverns, were not enough to accommodate the numerous dignitaries and congressmen along with their families and servants. On November 4, Congress adjourned and headed to Annapolis for its next convention and the Washingtons left for their beloved Mount Vernon in Virginia. For over four months, rural Princeton had enjoyed prestige and excitement. What prominence Princeton lost in the political arena would later be restored in the academic world.

In 1776, Bainbridge House was the headquarters of the British, and in 1783 it provided lodging for the Continental Congress. William Bainbridge, commander of the U.S.S. *Constitution* during the War of 1812, was born here in 1774.

The Barracks, the oldest house in Princeton, was not only occupied by British troops during the Revolution, it had also quartered them during the French and Indian Wars, as was mandatory for many Princeton residents—hence the name. The first Stockton in Princeton, "Richard the Settler," built the farmhouse in the 1690s using native fieldstone. The front portico and the right wing are modern additions.

Considered to be the most elegant of Princeton's country homes, Morven, at 55 Stockton Street, was the home of Richard and Annis Stockton. During the Revolution, Morven suffered extensive property destruction and plundering while the British occupied Princeton. Annis, a respected and published poet in her time, memorialized George Washington and the war in her epic poems.

Egyptian Revival statues guard the side entrance to Morven

Nassau Hall was entrenched in the activities of the Revolution from the beginning. The first State Legislature met here in 1776, approved the first State Constitution, inaugurated the first State governor, and adopted the State Seal. Throughout most of the war, the building was occupied by both British and American troops, respectively, who left it in shambles. After quick repairs, Nassau Hall briefly served as the capital of the new nation when the Continental Congress met here between June and November of 1783.

During the British occupation in 1776, General Cornwallis's troops built a fireplace inside the First Presbyterian Church (now Nassau Presbyterian Church), using the wooden pews and gallery rails as fuel. When the Continentals evicted the British in 1777, they also abused the church by first converting it into a barracks and later using it as a hospital. After the war, renovations and repairs enabled the 1783 college commencement to be held at the church again, with guests such as George Washington and the Continental Congress attending.

The original Stony Brook Bridge was made of wood with timber flooring. To keep the British from crossing the Stony Brook stream, the Americans attempted to destroy the bridge but were thwarted by the British. After the battle at Princeton, they were successful in pulling it down. This stone bridge was built in 1792 with a marker indicating the distance to Philadelphia and New York.

Princeton Battlefield State Park. At this site, American forces defeated a British brigade on January 3, 1777, eight days after their victory at Trenton on December 26, 1776. The eighty-five acre park remains very much as it was. Mercer Street, which cuts through the park, was not laid out until 1807. Today, the park contains the battlefield, the Thomas Clarke House, the Colonnade Monument, and the graves of American and British soldiers.

Monument to Hugh Mercer, who died in the Thomas Clarke farmhouse nine days after the Battle of Princeton. The farmhouse can be seen in the background.

Revolutionary re-enactors pose for a photo shoot in between events at Princeton Battlefield.

Quaker Thomas Clarke built his farmhouse in 1772 on land owned by his family since 1696. General Hugh Mercer, a Scottish physician and good friend of George Washington's, died here on January 12, 1777, nine days after being wounded at the Battle of Princeton. The Clarke house served as a hospital for both American and British troops. It now functions as a museum containing furnishings of the eighteenth century and exhibits pertaining to the Revolutionary War.

Thomas Clarke carriage barn.

Built in 1726 and rebuilt in 1760 following a fire, Stony Brook Friends Meeting House served as a barracks during the British occupation in 1776, and later as a hospital after the Battle of Princeton. Richard Stockton, "The Signer," is buried in the Quaker cemetery adjacent to the Meeting House, along with many of the first settlers of Princeton. The building closed in the mid-nineteenth century, but reopened in 1949.

Richard Stockton grave marker.

From the porch of the Thomas Olden House, Washington reportedly reviewed his troops on their way to Trenton. After the Battle of Princeton, he came again to request medical aid for the British Regulars that were wounded in the battle. Numerous homes in the surrounding area were opened as infirmaries for the wounded on both sides. As with most early colonial farmhouses, this home has been difficult to date, although 1696 has been suggested. It is now part of the estate of Drumthwacket, residence of the New Jersey governor, and serves as a gift shop.

Dated between 1702 and 1710, Rockingham is considered to be the second oldest house in the Millstone River Valley. From August to November 1783, George and Martha Washington rented the house, located in nearby Rocky Hill (now relocated to Rt. 603 in Kingston), for his headquarters while Congress was in session at Nassau Hall. During the Washingtons' occupation, Rockingham received many prominent guests. It has been completely restored to 1783 when the famous couple resided here.

The Colonnade Monument was erected from Ionic columns that had once adorned a nearby house. Passing through the memorial leads one to the common grave of 16 American and 21 British soldiers killed at the Battle of Princeton. A bronze plaque dedicated to the fallen soldiers lies above the grave, and is inscribed with the following lines by the English poet, Alfred Noyes:

> Here Freedom stood, by slaughtered friend and foe,
> And, ere the wrath paled or that sunset died.
> Looked through the ages; then, with eyes aglow,
> Laid them to wait that future side by side.

Revolutionary notables are buried in the oldest part of Princeton Cemetery. Among them are John Witherspoon, signer of the Declaration of Independence, and Aaron Burr, Jr., Vice President of the United States. Aaron Burr, Sr., the second president of the College of New Jersey, is buried near his son. A special section is cordoned off for Princeton University presidents.

Sculpted of limestone by Frederick W. MacMonnies, the Princeton Battle Monument was dedicated in 1922 by President Warren G. Harding. The memorial portrays Washington on horseback at the Battle of Princeton, Lady Liberty driving the soldiers to victory, a drummer boy, and the mortally wounded General Hugh Mercer.

Spirit of Place

Throughout Princeton's three-hundred-year history, architecture has documented the town's progression of growth and change, bequeathing a rich aesthetic heritage at the same time. Quintessential Princeton is a result of its diverse architecture; traditional and vernacular styles from every era are represented in town, gown, and township. A structure that dates from the late seventeenth century may stand next to its modern counterpart of the twenty-first century. Princeton's conservative side has not always approved of this co-mingling, but many believe it is a testament to the town's pride in its past and confidence in its future.

To preserve Princeton's living catalog of architecture, the Historic Preservation Review Committee of the Borough of Princeton has designated four historic districts: Jugtown, Bank Street, Mercer Hill, and Central. Each section is recognized for its uniqueness in culture, as well as architecture that contains many various styles: Federal, Greek Revival, Queen Anne, Gothic Revival, Second Empire, Italianate, Colonial Revival, and Vernacular. Jugtown, settled in 1695, is situated at the intersection of Harrison and Nassau Streets. At the beginning of the eighteenth century, houses, businesses, and a pottery works (hence its name) established this neighborhood. On Bank Street between Bayard Lane and Chambers Street, fancy gingerbread bric-a-brac decorates Queen Anne vernacular homes. Mercer Hill, the largest area designated by the historic committee, lies between Stockton and Mercer Streets and from Springdale Road to Dickinson Place. Noteworthy residences and public buildings are located in this section, including many houses built by Princeton's carpenter-builder, Charles Steadman. The Central Historic District, which runs along Nassau Street, includes the shopping district and the beginning of Princeton University's campus.

Historic Preservation in Princeton Township has designated areas representing the historical, agricultural, and industrial components of Princeton. They include Stony Brook Settlement (the first settlement) and Princeton Battlefield State Park, the Kingston Mill, Princeton Basin, and the Delaware and Raritan Canal Historic District. Some of the early farmhouses from the second half of the eighteenth century still stand in Princeton Township—they include Mansgrove, Maybury Hill, Castle Howard, and the Gulick-Hodge-Scott House, to name a few. Unlike Morven, most farmhouses began as simple, small structures erected strictly for shelter, only being enlarged as the owner's prosperity increased. Additions were then attached and facades altered to emulate the gracious Georgian manor, a style reflecting simple form and symmetry that was popularized by the wealthy plantation owners in the South.

Many prestigious architects have been commissioned to design high-style architecture for both town and gown. The term high-style refers to a design characterized by distinguishing details and elements, and usually, but not always, drawn by an architect. Renowned high-style architects in Princeton include Benjamin Henry Latrobe (the first professional architect in America), John McComb, Jr., Thomas Walter, John Notman, Richard Morris Hunt, Ralph Adams Cram (Princeton University's supervising architect from 1907 to 1929), the firm of McKim, Mead & White, Minoru Yamasaki, Ieoh Ming Pei, Rolf Bauhan, Michael Graves, and the firm of Venturi, Scott Brown & Associates.

Most architecture, however, is vernacular, even in Princeton. This designation refers to the more common dwellings usually built by a local carpenter-builder in a style either indigenous to the region or the era in which they were built. One of the most prolific builders of Princeton's vernacular architecture was Charles Steadman, a self-taught carpenter-builder who took his designs from pattern books published by professional architects. During the 1830s and 40s, Steadman constructed approximately seventy buildings combining Greek Revival and Federal elements, many of which still stand. John Notman, although a high-style architect, copied designs from Andrew Jackson Downing pattern books. His signature style, the Tuscan Villa, can be seen throughout Princeton.

Since Princeton University opened its doors in 1746, its architecture has spanned almost three centuries. Beginning with Nassau Hall's Georgian style, building design had followed prevailing trends until the end of the nineteenth century, when the trustees mandated that Collegiate Gothic should be the university's only architecture. With the passing of those trustees in the mid-twentieth century and new ones coming to power, Princeton's architectural program welcomed the popular contemporary mode that American architects had employed a decade earlier. A resurgence of interest in Frank Lloyd Wright brought a new modern movement: nature should dominate over structure, whereby buildings must conform to the contour of their surroundings and incorporate its materials. New buildings went up on campus to reflect this tenet, as did many off campus—Stuart Country Day School being a classic example. Architecture often comes full circle, however, which is evidenced at the university today. The newest building, Whitman College, is once more designed in Collegiate Gothic and should be completed in 2007. It will be a stunning addition to the campus.

Princeton architecture has attempted to keep pace with shifting tastes, sometimes to the outcry of traditionalists. The destruction of a still elegant building to make room for the newest design is hard to understand at times, but, in reflection, this is what has diversified Princeton. From the early classicism of Morven, with its simple symmetry of the eighteenth century, to the modern Stuart Country Day School with its aesthetic functionalism of the twentieth century, architecture in Princeton truly represents a spirit of place.

Princeton's Architecture

Although some fine examples of architectural styles in Princeton have been razed to make way for the new, most have been preserved. One method of preservation has been to move houses to new locations rather than tearing them down. For over two centuries, approximately one hundred houses in Princeton have been saved in this manner. Hence, we are able to appreciate the following styles of architecture.

English Vernacular (1680-1750)

As with most vernacular building in early America, the colonists used designs from the mother country and materials that were found on the premises. Only the wealthier plantations could afford to buy costlier supplies from England. Princeton's indigenous building sources consisted primarily of local fieldstone and red brick. Not until Greek Revival became popular in the early nineteenth century did Princeton façades change to wood.

The Houghton-Smith House was built c.1710-1715, with additions c.1760-75. According to the New Jersey Office of Historic Preservation, the oldest part of the house may be one of the few remaining "first generation" houses left in Princeton.

The ground floor stone walls of this house are believed to be from the original blacksmith shop. A 1749 survey suggests that this and the house next door stood on the same parcel. A second story was added c.1830-45.

Built of randomly laid local stone, probably c. 1750. There is at least one section in this house as well as the one in the previous photo that dates to the eighteenth century.

Georgian (1700-1780, locally to 1830)

The Georgian is a two-story symmetrical house formally arranged and embellished with simple classical elements. The paneled front door, placed in the center, may be surrounded with side pilasters, sidelights, a transom light, Palladian windows, pediments, and entablatures. Georgian houses in Princeton, however, exhibited fewer embellishments than in other areas in order to sustain the simplistic form.

Inn at Glencairn, 1736. The large, eighteenth-century Georgian section dwarfs the original seventeenth-century stone section. Today, the manor home is a bed and breakfast located three miles from downtown Princeton.

Maybury Hill (c.1725), was built as a 30 foot-square stone house with an attached kitchen. A later owner added a Georgian façade to combine both sections.

Richard Stockton built Morven on land that, in 1701, his grandfather purchased from William Penn. A fine example of early classicism, the original house was begun c.1755, although little of it remains today. Most of the present structure was built in the 1790s, with major alterations in the 1850s. The brick servants' quarters still stand in the rear. In 1954, Governor Walter Edge donated Morven to the State of New Jersey with the stipulation that it be used as a governor's mansion or a museum. Five governors lived here until the official governor's mansion became Drumthwacket in 1982.

Colross, a 1785 Georgian manor house, was moved from Virginia to Princeton, where it was rebuilt brick by brick.

Federal (1780-1820, locally to 1840)

The Federal style is very similar to Georgian, but may have wings on either side or added projections onto the back. The door surrounds were usually more elegant and detailed, with an elliptical fanlight and an elliptical arch or domed circular portico.

341 Nassau Street. Sitting at the corner of the Jugtown intersection (Nassau and Harrison Streets), this c.1800-1810 house was dubbed "Queens Court" while young girls preparing for admission to Evelyn College occupied it. Evelyn College (1887-1897) was the first women's college in New Jersey. It was a coordinate of Princeton University, attended by daughters of the faculty and sisters of male undergraduates.

The Nassau Club is a typical Georgian with Federal elements: slim columns, attached pilasters, and window muntins.

The Archibald Alexander House is located on the campus of the Theological Seminary. The house was not completed until 1821, before which time all cooking was done in the basement.

John Haviland designed Hodge House for the Theological Seminary in 1825. With its Palladian window and starburst heading, the house is more sophisticated than its counterpart, the Archibald Alexander House. Both houses' façades were originally unpainted brick.

Constructed as a three-bay house in 1830, The Manse was purchased in 1860 by the congregation of the First Presbyterian Church as a home for its pastor. It is speculated that the other two bays were added at the time of purchase.

The wing of this building, which contains a small door and only three windows, was probably built in the early eighteenth century. The main house, c.1830s, has the signature style of Charles Steadman.

The Woodrow Wilson House built by Charles Steadman in 1836; highlights include a handsome door and surround, an ornamental band under the eaves, and beautiful interior woodwork. The Wilson house is considered to be Steadman's best achievement.

Many of Princeton's fine Federal houses have survived.

Greek Revival (1825-1860)

Greek Revival public buildings feature the full-length temple columns of the Ionic, Doric, or Corinthian order that extend to a full entablature containing a pediment. Most Greek Revival houses, but not all, had porches with Doric or Ionic columns, sidelights, rectangular transoms, and pilasters.

Both Charles Steadman and Henry Laird built Alexander Street houses. As with most of his houses, Charles Steadman added Greek Revival columns to a side-hall Federal form, and like most New Jersey builders, he kept the gable to the side.

On Alexander Street is the house T.S. Elliot occupied while staying in Princeton.

Built in 1828 by Charles Steadman, this house originally stood on Nassau Street, next to the First Presbyterian Church, and was moved here in 1905. The wrought-iron fence and gate once stood in front of Nassau Hall.

Pilasters on the corners of this 1830s house, rare in Princeton, are attributed to Steadman.

A c.1830-40 Greek Revival with Italianate elements added later.

The central section of Drumthwacket was built c.1835 for Charles Smith Olden, New Jersey's governor during the Civil War. Moses Taylor Pyne bought the house in 1896; he expanded it to its present proportions and elegance with the aid of architect Raleigh C. Gildersleeve.

The Nassau Presbyterian Church in the evening.

A simple Greek Revival porch added onto a Federal style house.

Originally known as Sheldon House, this is a classic Greek form.

Gothic Revival (1840-1880)

The Gothic style ranged from picturesque board and batten houses to stone castles. Common features for the cottages included steeply pitched roofs, steep cross gables with gingerbread verge board trim, and windows that extended into the gable. Gothic in stone was very popular for churches and colleges.

John Notman designed Ivy Hall for Princeton University in 1846. After serving various functions through the years, it now belongs to Trinity Church.

In the mid-eighteenth century, Gothic emerged as the style of choice for many churches, particularly the Episcopalian. In 1845, the Parish School was the first Gothic component of Trinity Church to be built.

Princeton United Methodist Church.

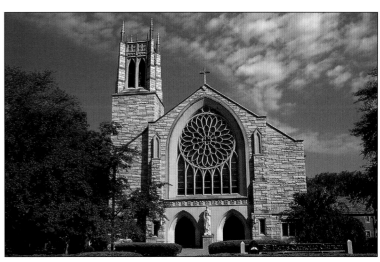

St. Paul's Catholic Church.

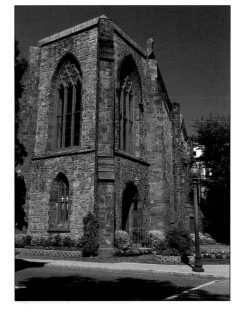

Nassau
Christian Center.

Richard Morris Hunt
designed this 1870s Gothic
Revival.

Italianate (1840-1885)

The Italianate style comprises two or three stories, sometimes with a tower attached to the two-story, sometimes asymmetrical, which is often referred to as the Italian or Tuscan Villa. Features include a low-pitched roof and tall, narrow windows sometimes grouped into threes with straight or rounded window headings.

Designed by John Notman in the Tuscan mode in 1850, Guernsey Hall was home to several prominent Princetonians. As with many of the large pre-twentieth century houses, it has been turned into a condominium.

An Italianate house with Stick style details decorating the porch, it was built in 1872. Recently it has been turned into a condominium.

Italianate houses abound on University Place.

Second Empire (1855-1885)

The Second Empire style is characterized by two or three stories with a mansard roof covered with slate or tin. Features include dormers in the roof, decorative brackets supporting the eaves, and arched windows with pediments. Second Empire can be simple or very elaborate.

There are many Second Empire homes throughout Princeton. These four photos show the various styles and sizes of the mode.

Stick (1860-1890)

Typically, the Stick style combined elements of Gothic Revival, taken primarily from Andrew Jackson Downing pattern books, and the forthcoming Queen Anne. Not many examples survive, as Stick elements can be easily removed.

Owned by the Princeton Theological Seminary, Lenox House, at 51 Library Place, is a good example of Stick elements and Victorian Gothic architecture. Richard Morris Hunt designed the house in 1870.

Queen Anne (1880-1910)

Not always loved, the Queen Anne sometimes wore rich colors, textures, and asymmetrical styling all on the same house. Almost every architectural element and form that had gone on before was represented somewhere on a Queen Anne. Today the style has its supporters and detractors, but all agree that it is something to talk about.

A Queen Anne with shingle siding, built c.1880-1890.

Bank Street has Victorian architecture on both sides of the street. This Queen Anne is a classic example.

Built between 1880 and 1890, this Queen Anne might have had more
Stick elements, which have since been removed.

Another Queen Anne with shingle siding that was built c. 1900-1910.

Shingle Style (1880-1900)

From top to bottom, the entire house, which is usually two or three stories, is clad in wood shingles. Other features include multi-gabled roofs, an asymmetrical façade, and porches.

A. Page Brown, of McKim, Mead & White, designed McCosh House, 387 Nassau Street, in 1887 for retired Princeton University President McCosh. Clad in shingles, it was an early example of Colonial Revival architecture in Princeton.

Also built by A. Page Brown of McKim, Mead & White (c.1887-1888), this 56 Bayard Lane house was one of the finest examples of the Shingle style in central New Jersey.

Colonial Revival (1880-1955)

Colonial Revival homes may contain many elements of colonial styling, particularly of Georgian and Federal. They usually feature a centered front door with one or all of the following features: portico, pediment, sidelights, and transom.

Many times, Colonial Revival features are out of proportion to the house. Some houses that are built to historical standards are indistinguishable from their earlier counterparts.

Door pediment to the Showcase House shown below.

Built in 1898, this Hodge Road house was the Junior League Showcase House for 2006.

Colonial Revival architecture at the beginning of the twentieth century.

1895 ⬤ 1995

Springdale Golf Club

Additional examples of early twentieth century Colonial Revival architecture.

A Dutch Colonial built c.1910-1920.

An unusual Spanish Revival built c. 1910-1920.

Tudor (1890-1940)

Although not found on all Tudors, the most distinguishing feature of this style is the decorative half-timbering on the exterior. Other features are tall, narrow windows with multi-pane glazing installed in multiple groups.

Renowned architect Raleigh Gildersleeve designed Lower Pyne in 1896 in the English timbered style of the sixteenth century.

Built for Professor Fine by Cope & Stewardson in 1898.

Between 1908 and 1909, all houses on FitzRandolph Rd. and Broadmead St. were built for Princeton University professors. As there was only one architect, the homogenous look became known as "White City."

International (1925-Present)

Distinguishing features of this style are the flat roof and smooth exterior walls. Originating in Europe, it considered functionalism to be paramount; aesthetics were not to be considered. American architects, working in a traditional trend in the United States, softened the starkness of the pure International house with gables, and used wood or stone instead of white stucco.

The home of Michael Graves, internationally famous architect.

Eclecticism (1880-1940)

A return to previous classical styles, although with more detailed and ostentatious adornments. A Beaux Arts roof may be flat, mansard, or gabled.

The Princeton Bank & Trust on Nassau Street, built in 1896, is Flemish Revival.

72

Built between 1900 and 1910, this Beaux Arts bank is on the corner of Nassau and Witherspoon Streets.

A Beaux Arts pediment at 201 Nassau Street, c. 1910-30.

Vernacular

Most architecture is vernacular and Princeton is no different in this regard. The following sampling illustrates modifications of high-style architecture.

This home was originally built c.1700 with additions in the eighteenth and nineteenth centuries; the main 3-bay section is c.1824.

Located at the intersection of Nassau and Harrison Streets, this 1730 house was typical of its day with a 3-bay side entry.

Built in 1850, this Vernacular Italianate building now houses a bookshop.

Charles Steadman built this 1832 house.

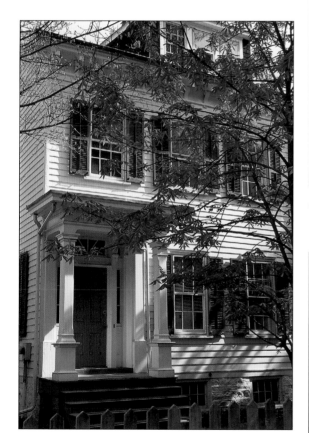

This mid-nineteenth century structure was Charles Steadman's last house.

The Monastery, 1860-1870, was named for unmarried faculty during the McCosh era in the third quarter of the nineteenth century.

Clearbrook Farm was built in the early 1800s.

An 1870 Vernacular Italianate.

This is possibly a Sears Catalog House that was popular for much of the twentieth century.

Built in 1958 by Rolf W. Bauhan, a prolific Princeton architect during the twentieth century, Mountain Lakes House is located on a 90-acre nature preserve. Bauhan designed the house to appear somewhat small on the outside, as was his trademark. It had six bedrooms and four fireplaces that were composed in six sections with as many roof lines. Today, the house is available for social and community functions.

These Hallowed Halls

Princeton's numerous learning institutions are renowned throughout the world. Along with Princeton University, the Institute for Advanced Study, Princeton Theological Seminary, and Westminster Choir College, there are several private elementary and secondary schools that bring students to the area.

Princeton University

Princeton University's tenure began in 1746 when two Presbyterian ministers, who later became the school's first and second presidents, requested a charter for the College of New Jersey. Classes began in Elizabeth at the home of President Jonathan Dickinson, where the first ten young men met to prepare themselves for entrance into the ministry. Upon Dickinson's death in 1747, the college moved to Newark at the parsonage of Aaron Burr, Sr. Because Newark was not convenient for the dominant Presbyterian community, eventually a new location was sought. The highly favored New Brunswick lost when several Prince Town Quaker families pooled their resources to meet the requirements of a thousand pounds, ten acres of cleared land, and two hundred acres of woodland for fuel. In the fall of 1756, Burr moved the college for the last time to Prince Town. One year later, Nassau Hall—where the entire college was housed until the beginning of the nineteenth century—opened its doors.

For the next one hundred years, the College experienced difficulties exacerbated by financial problems, agitated students, and a new attitude towards religion. As enrollment lagged, the College's growth did as well. When it lost its southern students during the Civil War, a major recruiting campaign concentrated on the North. Soon, a respectable student body returned, and with it a desire for Princeton to be on equal footing with New England schools emerged. For this, Princeton needed fresh blood. In 1868, it came directly from Scotland in the form of Reverend James Mc-Cosh, Princeton's eleventh president. When recruitment of the wealthy industrial north brought, in turn, generous alumni, funding became less of a problem, enabling McCosh to implement his ideas. When he retired in 1888, the campus had greatly increased in acreage and amount of buildings erected, students and faculty had more than doubled, and prospective students were applying from around the country. The college's renewed program needed a new name to fit its exalted reputation. In 1896, the College of New Jersey became Princeton University.

This set the stage for the next innovative president, Woodrow Wilson. In his quest to put Princeton on a higher intellectual plain, Wilson looked to England, adopting from that country the preceptorial system, whereby preceptors guided small groups of students to work independently. He also initiated the studies program: two years of required courses in the arts and sciences, followed by two years of a major study—a plan used by most colleges today. And he implemented the honor system during examinations, becoming the third college to do so. Residential colleges, however, the program that was to deter the inequitable eating clubs and for which he fought for the hardest, did not come to fruition until much later. Wilson did not live to see that there are now five residential colleges to house all freshmen and sophomores, each with approximately 500 students. They are a testament to Wilson's vision of imparting a sense of community and his desire to coalesce diversity among students. By the end of his eight-year term in 1910, Wilson had elevated Princeton to a world-renowned institution of higher learning, where it has remained ever since.

In 1756, Nassau Hall, the largest public building in the colonies, was built by architect Robert Smith, who wanted to use brick. The frugal trustees said no. Instead, it was built from local stone, resulting in a rusticity and simplicity that gives it a more provincial look. Renovations after fires in 1802 and 1855 have greatly changed the initial structure so that only the Faculty Room, although it too has been altered slightly, retains its original integrity. Nassau Hall is one of the few extant American structures still serving the purpose for which it was originally intended. Most notables of the colonial era have crossed its threshold, followed by nearly every President of the United States. Today it houses the administrative offices, which include the President's office.

Maclean House. Concurrent with his work on Nassau Hall in 1756, Robert Smith built the president's house, which served as the residence for all college presidents until 1879. In 1968, it became the home of the Alumni Council and was renamed in honor of John Maclean, founder of the Alumni Association. A few renovations have altered the exterior: the roof was raised and a dormer inserted; a bay window and a porch were added; and the brick, which the trustees allowed this time, has since been painted yellow. The chimneys and window-glass are original and the interior is intact, maintaining its fine paneling.

Built in 1837, the Joseph Henry House has moved three times to finally rest northeast of Nassau Hall. The home's design has been attributed to Henry himself, who not only had a distinguished career as a physicist, but also taught an elective course in architecture. Today's exterior is the result of modern renovations. In 1846, Professor Henry left for Washington D.C. to become director and secretary of the new Smithsonian Institution. Since 1973, the house has been the official residence of the Dean of the University Faculty.

In 1803, Benjamin Latrobe designed Stanhope Hall (originally called Geological Hall), and its twin, Philosophical Hall (razed in 1873). These two buildings stood opposite each other flanking Nassau Hall, which gave the growing campus symmetry and reinforced the symmetrical attributes of its buildings. Recently, it has been home to campus communications and security offices.

Designed in Venetian Gothic Revival in 1873, Chancellor Green Hall was the first commission by nineteen-year-old William A. Potter, and the first to be built specifically as a library. The central section, a two-story octagonal rotunda for storing most of the books, is topped with a stunning stained-glass octagonal skylight in the dome. Fifteen years later, when Chancellor's books were overflowing, Potter built East Pyne Library in Collegiate Gothic, attaching it to Chancellor via a passageway known as the "hyphen." Chancellor was retained as a reading room until Firestone Library was built in 1948, replacing both Chancellor and Pyne. Set for the wrecking ball at times, Chancellor's immediate future is safe, as the rotunda's dome has been recently cleaned and restored.

Once the college library, East Pyne has been renovated to house classrooms and offices of the university's foreign literature departments.

A stone carving of James McCosh, past college president, stands guard near the entrance to East Pyne.

Statue of John Witherspoon outside East Pyne.

Stained glass in the "hyphen," which connects
Chancellor Green Hall and East Pyne.

Built in 1836, possibly by John Notman, West College was Princeton's second dormitory. In 1926, it was remodeled
on its west side in Colonial Revival. The arcade was added at that time and the university store occupied the ground
floor. Since 1964, it has housed the Office of Admissions.

Clio Hall (shown here) and Whig Hall were homes to the oldest college literary and debating clubs in America, the American Whig Society (1769) and the Cliosophic Society (1770). During the nineteenth century, rivalry between the two societies was very intense; students could be a member of only one club and could not enter the other's building. In 1928, the two merged and moved into Whig Hall. During the clubs' two-hundred year history, Whig-Clio alumni have gone on to become federal and state supreme court justices, U.S. representatives, college presidents, senators, and U.S. presidents. A. Page Brown erected these marble structures in 1889.

The imposing entrance to Clio Hall.

Whig Hall.

Designed in 1877, Witherspoon Hall dormitory was considered the most beautiful in the world at the time. Since then, it has been both derided and applauded, depending on one's view of Victorian architecture; the entire repertoire of such architecture is represented in this one building. Witherspoon's five stories and impressive tower (since removed) were intended to attract affluent students from the north. It had many amenities, including dumbwaiters and water closets on every floor.

President McCosh took a personal interest in the landscaping of the campus, laying out paths and selecting building sites. McCosh Walk begins through the arch in the corner of McCosh Court and ends here at the Tiger Gateway between Blair and Stafford Little Halls.

Designed by Cope and Stewardson in 1899, Stafford Little Hall is the university's second Collegiate Gothic building. It follows the boundary line of the campus as it was before the removal of the train station. Stafford's charm emanates from its Flemish gables, Tudor chimneys, crenellated tower, and fashionable bays.

Murray-Dodge Hall. Built in 1879 in the Romanesque style, Murray Hall housed the Philadelphia Society, the oldest religious organization in the country. As the Society grew, it added Dodge Hall in 1900 in the new Collegiate Gothic style. Dodge Hall was connected to Murray with a 52-foot covered walkway, giving the complex continuity: in addition, the same brownstone on Murray was used for Dodge, and a renovated Gothic roof was applied to Murray. Today, Dodge is the center of religious activities and Murray is home to "Theatre Intime," where James Stewart, José Ferrer, and Joshua Logan discovered their talents.

Murray Hall's "Theatre Intime."

Erected in 1907, McCosh Hall was the largest building on campus designed for Woodrow Wilson's revolutionary idea of preceptorial instruction. The building contains a large lecture room accommodating 600 students, two smaller rooms for 250 each, and one that holds 150. There are also faculty and recitation rooms and nine separate entrances to ease the flow of changing classes.

Tympanum over the main entrance to University Chapel (shown below). As described by St. John in Revelations, Jesus is seated wearing the golden crown and supported by two angels. The symbols are four animals representing the Evangelists: the lion is Mark, the angel is Mathew, the eagle is John, and the ox is Luke.

The Mather Sundial, which sits in McCosh Court, was given to the university in 1907 by Sir William Mather, governor of Victoria University in Manchester, England, to symbolize the relationship between Princeton and Oxford and between America and Great Britain. For years, only privileged seniors could sit on the steps of the sundial. McCosh and Dickinson Halls and the University Chapel form three sides of the court.

Designed by R. A. Cram, University Chapel was built between 1925 and 1928. It is the third largest college church in the world and thought to be one of the most beautiful Gothic buildings in America. The Chapel seats almost two thousand and accommodates eleven denominations.

Tympanum over the chapel's west entrance. A pair of "grotesques" are located on either side of the entry portal. On the right is the head of Cram, the architect; on the left is his assistant.

University Chapel interior.

Firestone Library was the fifth building to house the main library when it opened in 1948. In order that the chapel remains the tallest building on campus, the library extends substantially underground. It is the largest open-stack research library in the world and has the highest per-student circulation of any university library in the United States. Together, Firestone and its satellite repositories contain nearly eight million volumes. When the site was excavated in 1946, a bonanza of fossilized fish was discovered. Deemed to be a great find by the American Museum of Natural History, the fossils can be seen in Guyot Hall.

Architects Day and Klauder designed both Holder and Madison Halls in 1910 in the Collegiate Gothic style. They are now part of Rockefeller College, residential dormitories for freshman and sophomores. Holder's 140-foot tower fashioned after Canterbury Cathedral is a visible landmark in town. While Holder contains the dormitories, Madison Hall is the dining commons for all Rockefeller College.

Holder door on Nassau Street.

Bikes in Holder cloister.

Madison Hall.

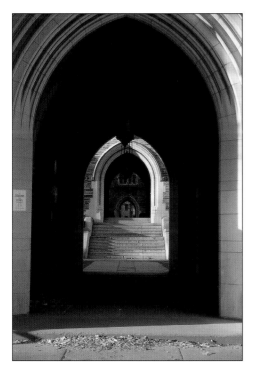

Joline-Campbell Hall Arch. In 1932, Joline Hall, designed by Charles Klauder, was attached to Campbell Hall, designed by the Cram firm in 1909. Both dormitories belong to Mathey College. An arch connects Campbell to Blair Hall, while a vista of arches runs from Campbell to Nassau Street.

The university's ubiquitous bikes in Joline-Blair Arch.

Watchful tiger on Joline-Campbell Arch.

Built in 1924, Forbes College was originally the Princeton Inn until the university bought it in 1970. An addition designed by Robert Venturi integrated the requirements needed for space while maintaining the charm of the old hotel, thus creating a residential college for undergraduates.

Saying goodbye at the University Book Store.

Looking up from the entrance of the southern campus to Nassau Hall's steeple.

Designed in 1922 by Ralph Adams Cram in Venetian Gothic, McCormick Hall houses the Department of Art and Archeology. Since Cram, numerous additions and alternations have given critics much to lament. Exterior criticisms notwith-standing, the art collection is sterling. Of particular interest are the Boudinot Rooms pertaining to the Revolutionary War period.

Built in 1849, Prospect illustrates the typically asymmetrical and romantic Italianate style so favored by its architect, John Notman. In 1878, the house was donated to the college for use as the residence of its presidents. The gardens laid out behind the house by Mrs. Woodrow Wilson are still maintained. Prospect has been used as a faculty club since 1968, when the official presidential residence moved off-campus into the Lowrie House. A beautiful glass and concrete addition houses the Garden and Tap Rooms that look out over the gardens.

Lovely Prospect gardens in spring.

1879 Hall was a dormitory that was popular with upperclassmen, as it was close to the eating clubs. Built in 1904 in Tudor Gothic, it has functioned as administrative offices since 1960.

Frist Campus Center. Venturi, Scott Brown renovated the 1908 three-story Tudor Gothic building, turning it into a first-class social center for Princeton students that opened in 2000. It includes a common area with a convenience store and convenience services, dining lounges, a lecture hall, a theatre, a library, and much more.

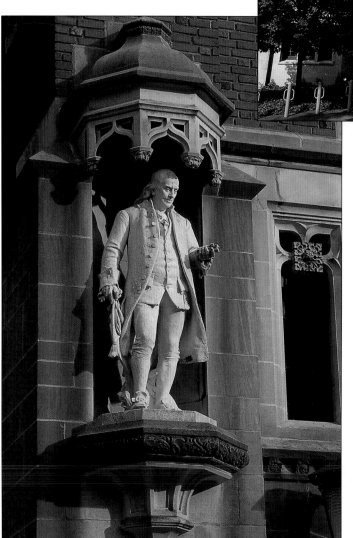

Benjamin Franklin stands guard at the north entrance to Frist Campus Center.

Built in 1909 for the sciences and geology, Guyot Hall seems like a dinosaur itself; on the exterior, two hundred gargoyles introduce visitors to the biology section on the east and the geology section on the west. A Natural History Museum and the impressive Geosciences Library are found inside.

Dod Hall is an upper-class dormitory that has been praised by students for its light and airy rooms, but criticized by architects for its location; it stands in the viewing line from Nassau Hall to the athletic fields. It was built in the Romanesque Revival design in 1890.

Florentine style Brown Hall was, along with Alexander Hall, the last architectural variation attempted by the university before the advent of the Collegiate Gothic mode. Built in 1892, Brown is the fourth in the line of dormitories. The flooding of natural daylight through the oversized and generous windows more than compensated for its plain style.

Cuyler Hall is an upper class dormitory designed in 1912 by Day and Klauder in the Collegiate Gothic style. Although it is Princeton's smallest dormitory, it is considered one of the handsomest.

Gothic Patton Hall was built in 1906.

Dillon Gymnasium gargoyle.

Constructed in 1947, Dillon Gymnasium is one of the last buildings on campus built in the Collegiate Gothic style. Dillon has crenellated towers and is also the last building to be dressed with carved gargoyles. U.S. Senator Bill Bradley, class of 1965, led the basketball team to its highest excellence by winning three successive league championships.

Although not architecturally significant, Pyne Hall looks lovely when the magnolias are in bloom.

Magnolia trees are plentiful on campus. Here they complement Henry Hall beautifully.

Pyne Hall arches looking up to University Place.

I. M. Pei built Spelman Halls in 1973. A modernist architect, Pei devised two triangles that make up fifty-eight apartments, each containing living and dining areas, complete kitchen, bath, an outside balcony, and four private bedrooms.

Beautiful magnolia trees line Blair Walk, which leads from the main campus to the railroad station.

Stone carving of St. Michael
on Foulke Hall.

On Henry Hall opposite St. Michael, St.
George slays the dragon.

Built in 1913, the Class of 1887 Boathouse is home to Princeton's crew team and the 2004 Olympic team. Princeton participated in competitive rowing starting in 1870, and team members trained on the narrow Delaware and Raritan Canal. When barge traffic became hazardous, however, the sport was dropped until the Millstone River was dammed in 1906 to create Lake Carnegie.

Robertson Hall. The Woodrow Wilson School of Public and International Affairs was founded in 1930 to support the disciplines of history, economics, politics, and sociology to prepare students for public service. In 1966, Minoru Yamasaki designed a pure white ensemble of entablature, pedestal, and fifty-eight concrete pillars cast in quartz to attempt a new classicism. It was dedicated by university president Robert F. Goheen and President Lyndon B. Johnson.

The Fountain of Freedom, which stands in the reflecting pool in
Scudder Plaza. Robertson Hall is in the background.

Built in 1917 as an eating club, this Collegiate Gothic style building has been purchased by the university and now houses Bendheim Center for Finance.

The rich color and texture of Fisher Hall, designed by Venturi, Scott Brown in 1991, complements the stark white of Robertson Hall next door. Fisher houses economic studies.

The Computer Science Building contains 57,000 square feet of classrooms, research laboratories, lecture hall, administrative offices, and seminar rooms; it was built in 1989 by Kliment and Halsband Architects.

Located on Prospect Avenue, the imposing Ferris S. Thompson Gateway designed by McKim, Mead, & White in 1911 was the entrance to University Field, the original baseball field. It was moved in the 1950s to facilitate construction of the Engineering Quad. Of the two gates by McKim, Mead, & White on campus, this is considered the most impressive.

The French style villa previously called Arbor Inn was the last eating club to be built in 1923. It is now owned by the university and houses the Center for Study of Religion.

CENTER FOR
JEWISH LIFE

70 Washington Road

The Center for Jewish Life, built in 1993 by Robert A. M. Stern, Dean of Yale's Architecture School, was the university's attempt to mitigate anti-Semitism, an effort that has seen fruition with this building. Designed in keeping with the eating clubs around the corner, the Center was built to accommodate the religious, social, education, and dietary needs of Princeton's Jewish community.

Eating Clubs on Prospect Avenue

When Greek-letter fraternities were banned in 1855, development of another form of socializing was inevitable. In 1879, upperclassmen rented the vacant Ivy Hall on Mercer Street and hired personnel to serve as cooks. A few years later, Ivy Club received the university's permission to build a facility off-campus. With financial help from alumni, architects were hired to build a stunning mansion that became the paradigm for all other clubs that followed. As the clubs increased, so did the competition to join. By 1906, fourteen clubs had inducted almost three-quarters of the upperclassmen, leaving a small minority out. This appalled University President Woodrow Wilson, who began a never-ending debate over the desirability of the clubs. Wilson wanted the eating clubs to convert to residential quadrangles or colleges, because this would dissolve class distinctions and exclusive social cliques, freeing the mind for the capacity to learn. During the course of the twentieth century, membership has vacillated, as students have boycotted the clubs from time to time. Out of twenty original clubs, there are eleven remaining at last count.

1916 Gothic Tower Club.

The entrance to Tower Club.

What Cannon Club, built in 1910, lacks in adornment it more than makes up for with interest, as a cannon sits on the front lawn. The university had at one time acquired Cannon Club as an office for the University Writing Center, but Princeton alumni have recently repurchased the building.

Quadrangle Club, designed in 1916 by trustee H. O. Milliken, is an elegant Georgian Revival. His lack of study is apparent in the over-scaled portico that does not fit the façade.

Designed in Tudor Gothic by Cope and Stewardson in 1896, Ivy Club was the first off-campus structure to be built for upperclass clubs and was "detached and breathlessly aristocratic," as noted by F. Scott Fitzgerald.

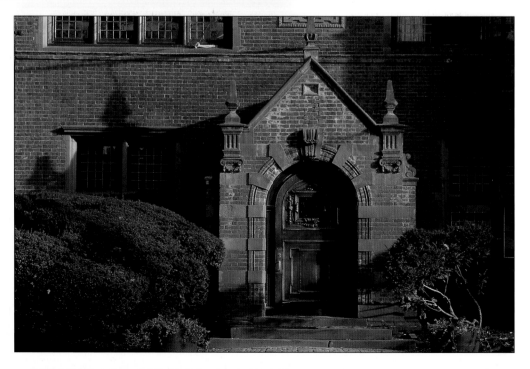

In 1906, ten years after Ivy Club stunned the trustees, McKim, Mead, and White designed a striking Georgian Revival for Cottage Club, the second oldest eating club.

Colonial Club was built in 1907 as a Colonial Revival. The oversized entry portico with its four massive Ionic columns is used for events that can be observed from the street.

Designed by Mellor and Meigs in 1914, Charter Club is a beautiful Georgian manor. Its favorite undergraduate had to be actor James Stewart ('32).

The charming Cloister Inn, a Collegiate Gothic designed in 1923.

Princeton Graduate School

Although not formally implemented, Princeton's Graduate School had very early beginnings with James Madison as the first graduate student in 1771. University President James McCosh laid out a graduate school plan in 1868, but not until 1900 was a college officially established. In 1913, the architectural firm of Cram, Goodhue, and Ferguson built the first graduate facility in the country, making Princeton a true university. The Collegiate Gothic design, fashioned after Cambridge and Oxford, and Beatrix Farrand's landscaping invoke quietude and spirituality.

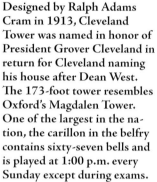

Designed by Ralph Adams Cram in 1913, Cleveland Tower was named in honor of President Grover Cleveland in return for Cleveland naming his house after Dean West. The 173-foot tower resembles Oxford's Magdalen Tower. One of the largest in the nation, the carillon in the belfry contains sixty-seven bells and is played at 1:00 p.m. every Sunday except during exams.

The much smaller Pyne Tower, which contains the living quarters of the administrator in residence, sits at the southwest corner of the quadrangle. On the first floor of the tower is a vestibule graced with a large fireplace and a memorial window honoring six graduate students who lost their lives in World War I. Cleveland tower is in the background.

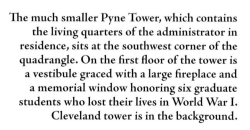

Upon entering Proctor Dining Hall, designed by Ralph Adams Cram in 1913, one senses spirituality rather than academia. A beautiful stained glass masterpiece by William Willet watches over the High Table, where prayers would be said before meals. An organ, refurbished during the 1960s, completes the spiritual tone.

The bronze figure of Andrew Fleming West, first dean of the graduate school, sits in the lovely Thomson College Court. Each suite in the dormitories has its own fireplace.

In 1913, Ralph Adams Cram designed Wyman House, official residence of the dean of the graduate school, in a low-keyed Tudor style.

Princeton Theological Seminary

Founded in 1812, Princeton Theological Seminary was the first Presbyterian institution to be established in the United States. Prior to the nineteenth century, nearly all colleges were founded by Protestant denominations for the purpose of educating young men for the ministry. Along with divinity, studies consisted of the classics, law, and medicine. By the end of the eighteenth century, however, the enlightenment period that had been forged in Europe brought radical theories to American colleges. As a result of changing attitudes, the emergence of scientific studies that increased the curriculum, and a sudden migration to the west that left a shortage of clergy, the Presbyterian General Assembly decided that a separate divinity school was needed. They would establish a postgraduate school in theology that met the approval of the trustees of the College of New Jersey.

The assembly elected a board of directors who, in turn, appointed a professor for the new college. In 1812, classes for three students were launched in the home of Professor Alexander. As enrollment grew, students were transferred to Nassau Hall at the college until Princeton Theological Seminary's first building, Alexander Hall, was erected. Richard Stockton, son of the Commodore, donated three acres on today's Mercer Street for the campus. The seminary is located on more than thirty acres today, covering a section on which the Battle at Princeton was fought. It maintains ties to the university, and still holds commencement exercises in the University Chapel.

With the seminary's formation, its founders decreed that religion without education and education without religion would eventually harm the church. This doctrine encouraged the seminary to strive for excellence in education and theology, putting an emphasis on personal salvation, repentance, forgiveness, and the teachings of Jesus Christ. Because these tenets formed the foundation of Protestant American religion—whether of the Puritan, Calvinist, Lutheran, Quaker, Wesleyan, or liberal Reformation practices—the seminary became desirable as a training center for church leaders of all faiths, specializing in preaching, evangelism, and missions. Princeton Theological Seminary today is a denominational school with an ecumenical constituency that serves worldwide and has produced more than fourteen thousand men and women graduates.

John McComb Jr., who designed New York's City Hall and Old Queens at Rutgers, designed Alexander Hall. Completed in 1818, "Old Seminary" housed all aspects of seminary life—classrooms, library, dining, lodging, and chapel. In its Georgian style it is similar to Nassau Hall, but better proportioned. Today, it is used as a dormitory except for the room that was the original chapel, which is still used for prayer meetings and group activities.

Designed by J. P. Huber, Brown Hall is built in the Georgian style except for its neoclassical portico. The building opened in 1865 as a dormitory, through the generosity of Mrs. Isabella Brown, a Southern sympathizer. Tales of Southern prisoners being allowed to enroll at the Seminary and to attend classes in uniform so impressed Mrs. Brown, she renewed her gift. The renovation of Brown's exterior in 1994 was awarded first prize for excellence in historical preservation by the New Jersey Historical Commission.

Designed in the Venetian Gothic style by William A. Potter in 1876, Stuart Hall houses lecture rooms. It has recently been renovated to include the latest media technology and a computer resource center, while at the same time retaining its original architectural integrity.

Hodge Hall. Mrs. Stuart, who donated the granite and brownstone dormitory in 1893, suggested the crescent shape to the architect, R.H. Robertson, so that every room would receive sunlight at some point during the day. Renovations in 1989 included first-floor offices for the faculty and dormitory rooms on the upper three floors. Recently, the exterior mortar has been restored to its original color.

Built in 1834 by Charles Steadman, Miller Chapel was named for Dr. Samuel Miller, the Seminary's second professor. The chapel was adorned with stained glass windows in 1874. Originally facing Mercer Street, it was moved to its present location in 1933, where it was enlarged and its stained glass windows were removed.

Richard Morris Hunt designed Lenox House in 1878 as part of the Arts and Crafts movement; it now houses research such as the Dead Sea Scrolls Project.

Designed by Rolf W. Bauhan for the Hun School, Roberts Hall is built in three sections. The center section was originally used as classrooms and the sides as dormitories. The Seminary acquired Roberts Hall in 1943; since then it has been used as apartments for married students.

Speer Library opened in 1957. Above the entrance are two limestone columns containing twelve symbols, each of which represents an important Christian truth. The building holds 400,000 volumes, the library's circulation offices, two classrooms, and the Reference Department.

Built in 1989, Templeton Hall is the newest academic facility on the Seminary's original campus. Replicating an eighteenth-century building, Templeton contains classrooms, administrative offices, and a state-of-the-art communications and media center.

Springdale has been the residence of the Seminary president since 1903. Built in 1851 by Commodore Robert Stockton for his son, Richard, its architecture has been attributed to John Notman. Looking similar to a design from an Andrew Jackson Downing pattern book, Springdale is a picturesque delight combining Italianate and Gothic elements.

The Archibald Alexander House, situated to the right of Alexander Hall facing Mercer Street, is named for the first professor of the Seminary, who resided here from 1818 until his death in 1851.

Standing to the left of Alexander Hall facing Mercer Street, Hodge House was designed by John Haviland for the Seminary's third professor, Dr. Charles Hodge; it was completed in 1825.

Institute for Advanced Study

The cultivation of ideas, speculative research, and the pursuit of knowledge for its own sake comprised the concepts on which the Institute for Advanced Study was created in 1930. Alexander Flexner, the founding director, conceived and developed the theories that culminated in the building of the first residential institute for advanced study in the United States. But it was the funds provided by philanthropists Louis Bamberger and his sister, Caroline Bamberger Fuld, which made it possible. The Institute soon became one of the world's leading centers for theoretical research and intellectual inquiry. During the 1930s, it provided a safe haven for scholars fleeing Europe, Albert Einstein among them. Einstein remained at the Institute for Advanced Study until his death in 1955.

Today, the Institute offers its permanent faculty and visiting members freedom to pursue fundamental scholarly work that will make significant contributions to a broad range of fields in the sciences and humanities. Work takes place in four schools: Historical Studies, Mathematics, Natural Sciences, and Social Science. A permanent faculty of twenty-six eminent scholars guides the work of the schools, and each year awards fellowships to some one hundred and ninety visiting members from about one hundred universities and research institutions throughout the world.

Fuld Hall, constructed in 1939, was named for Felix Fuld, Caroline Bamberger Fuld's husband and business partner of Louis Bamberger (of the department store chain). Designed by Jens F. Larson in the neo-Georgian style so popular in the 1930s, Fuld Hall contains faculty and administrative offices, the Mathematics and Natural Sciences Library, and the Common Room, where Institute members and faculty gather for tea each afternoon.

Built in 1993, Wolfensohn Hall is used for lectures, films, and concerts.

Across the Institute Pond, Simonyi Hall houses the School of Mathematics.

Elyn Zimmerman sculpture. In 2005, Elyn Zimmerman sculpted three granite benches, with accompanying large columns, for the occasion of the Institute's 75th anniversary. Each bench holds an inscription to commemorate three prominent people in the history of the Institute. One is dedicated to Albert Einstein, one is for Abraham Flexner (Founding Director of IAS), and one is for George Kennan, a faculty member.

Olden Farm (originally called Olden Manor). William Olden, one of the founding families of the Stony Brook settlement, built his home on this site in 1697. The size of the western wing of the current house indicates that it probably encloses the original structure. The middle section was added in the late eighteenth century and the east side dates to the mid-nineteenth century. Today, it is the residence of the Director of the Institute for Advanced Study.

Princeton's Schools

Westminster Choir College. World-renowned for educating men and women at both undergraduate and graduate levels for careers in church music, teaching, and performance, the Choir has performed around the world since 1929. In 1980, it was the first to be featured in the "Live from Lincoln Center" series and recently it participated in the ten-thousandth performance of the New York Philharmonic. Westminster Choir College merged with Rider College in 1992.

Princeton High School was established in 1899; the main section was built in 1928. The school has received top honors in mathematics and science competitions. Many seniors have received National Merit Scholarship semifinal or commended scholar's recognition, and more than eighty percent of students attend four-year colleges, half of which are Ivy League schools.

Princeton Day School, a private school for grades K-12, was established when Miss Fine's School for Girls (1894) and Princeton Country Day School for boys (1924) merged in 1965. The school owns two buildings that were once part of two different estates: Pretty Brook Farm (left), owned by Dean Mathey who left most of his property and farmhouse to Princeton Country Day School, and Colross (right), a 1785 Georgian manor house.

Stuart Country Day School of the Sacred Heart is one of a few schools in New Jersey committed to the education of girls from grades Preschool through 12. In 1963, renowned architect Jean Labatut designed the school to lie within the rugged contour of the land. Composed of roughened concrete and green-glazed brick, it repeats its natural surroundings. The newest addition, Cor Unum, a performance and gathering space, was designed by Robert Venturi, a student of Labatut's, and echoes the elements found in the original architecture of the school.

Hun School was founded in 1914 as a math tutorial school for Princeton University undergraduates. In 1925, it acquired the mansion Edgerstoune. During the following years, the school expanded into a college preparatory program, with new buildings added for classes, dining, boarding, athletics, and student activities.

Hun School Academic Center.

Hun School's lovely grounds.

Princeton Academy of the Sacred Heart, founded in 1998, enrolls 217 boys. Rolf W. Bauhan built the Tudor mansion called Highland House in 1930 for Mr. & Mrs. Thomas Dignan. Containing twenty-two rooms, the first floor includes elaborate hand-carved paneling, beams, and banisters. Stained glass windows depict King Arthur and the Knights of the Round Table, as well as the Princeton University Crest. Today, the house serves as the admissions office and the gathering place for special events.

The American Boychoir School. Architect Harrie Lindeberg built the previously known Albemarle between 1913 and 1917 for George B. Lambert. Frederick Law Olmstead designed the grounds and gardens. In 1950, Columbus Boychoir purchased the estate and subsequently changed the name to the now famous American Boychoir School.

The Lewis School was founded in 1973 to provide education for dyslexic children from pre-school through high school and college preparatory. The large stone mansion, originally called Thanet Lodge, was built in the late nineteenth century.

Saint Joseph's Seminary began as a college preparatory school in 1914 to educate Roman Catholic men for the priesthood. It now functions as a formation center for education and also hosts retreats for adults and youths of all religions.

A Gothic building on the campus of Saint Joseph's Seminary.

Frances Chapin, who believed that education should encompass the whole child—emotional, physical, social, and moral, not just educational—founded Chapin School in 1931. After Chapin's death in 1951, the students' parents carried on her vision by establishing a corporation to operate the school. The middle section of the PK-8 school is part of the 1740 Henry D. Phillips house.

Ferdinand Durang built Saint Joseph's chapel from a design in 1934.

Bibliography

Bill, Alfred Hoyt. *A House Called Morven: Its Role in American History . . .* Revised by Constance M. Greiff, with a postscript by Bolton F. Schwartz. Princeton, NJ: Princeton University Press, 1978.

Bill, Alfred Hoyt. *New Jersey and the Revolutionary War.* Princeton, NJ: D. Van Nostrand Company, Inc., 1964.

Blumenson, John J. G. *Identifying American Architecture: A Pictorial Guide to Styles and Terms, 1600-1945.* New York: W. W. Norton & Co., 1981.

Collins, V. Lansing. *Princeton Past and Present.* Revised edition. Princeton, NJ: Princeton University Press, 1945.

Croll, Emily. "Craftsmanship, Comfort, and Elegance: The Architecture of Rolf W. Bauhan, 1920-1966." *Princeton History Number Fifteen,* 1998.

Cunningham, John T. *New Jersey: America's Main Road.* Garden City, New York: Doubleday & Co., Inc., 1976.

Derry, Ellis L. *Old and Historic Churches of New Jersey, Volume 2.* Medford, NJ: Plexus Publishing, Inc., 1994.

Di Ionno, Mark. *A Guide to New Jersey's Revolutionary War Trail for Families and History Buffs.* New Brunswick, NJ: Rutgers University Press, 2000.

Einstein, Albert. *The New Quotable Einstein.* Collected and ed. Alice Calaprice. Princeton and Oxford: Princeton University Press, 2005.

Gambee, Robert. *Princeton.* New York: W. W. Norton & Company, 1987.

Gooding, Cynthia, Photographs by Mercedes Rogers. *A Princeton Guide: Walks, Drives & Commentary.* Somerset, NJ: The Middle Atlantic Press, 1971.

Gowans, Alan. *Architecture in New Jersey.* Princeton, NJ: D. Van Nostrand Company, Inc., 1964.

Greiff, Constance M., Mary W. Gibbons, and Elizabeth G. C. Menzies. *Princeton Architecture: A Pictorial History of Town and Campus.* Princeton, NJ: Princeton University Press, 1967.

Greiff, Constance M. & Wanda S. Gunning. *Morven: Memory, Myth & Reality.* Princeton, NJ: Historic Morven, Inc., 2004.

Guter, Robert P. & Janet W. Foster, photographs by Jim DelGiudice. *Building By The Book: Pattern-Book Architecture in New Jersey.* New Brunswick, NJ: Rutgers University Press, 1992.

Hand, Susanne C. *New Jersey Architecture.* Trenton: New Jersey Historical Commission, Department of State, 1995.

Princeton Township Historic Preservation Commission. *Historic Preservation in Princeton Township: A Brief History of Princeton.* www.princetontwp.org/histofpt. html.(February 9, 2005)

McAlester, Virginia & Lee. *A Field Guide to American Houses.* New York: Alfred A. Knopf, 2000.

McCormick, Richard P. *New Jersey from Colony to State – 1609-1789.* Princeton, NJ: D. Van Nostrand Company, Inc., 1964.

Menzies, Elizabeth G. C. "General Washington's Highway Route 27-206," *Princeton History Number Two,* 1977.

Rhinehart, Raymond P., photographs by Walter Smalling Jr. *Princeton University.* New York: Princeton Architectural Press, 2000.

Schmidt, George P. *Princeton and Rutgers: The Two Colonial Colleges of New Jersey.* Princeton, NJ: D. Van Nostrand Company, Inc., 1964.

Woodward, Ruth L. *A Journey of Faith For One Hundred and Fifty Years: A History of the Princeton United Methodist Church.* 1997.

Index